Mc Graw Hill **Children's Publishing**

This edition published in the United States of America in 2003 by
McGraw-Hill Children's Publishing,
a Division of The McGraw-Hill Companies
8787 Orion Place
Columbus, Ohio 43240-4027

www.MHkids.com

Library of Congress Cataloging-in-Publication Data is on file with the publisher.

© Autumn Publishing Ltd 2003

Printed in China.

1-57768-558-X

1 2 3 4 5 6 7 8 9 10 BRI 09 08 07 06 05 04 03

GETTING DOWN TO BUSINESS

WATERBIRD BOOKS

Columbus, Ohio

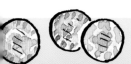

First published in 2003 by Brimax,
an imprint of Autumn Publishing Ltd,
Appledram Barns, Chichester PO20 7EQ

Created by Nimbus Books
Written by Lorraine Horsley
Illustrated by John Eastwood

Edited in the U.S. by Joanna Callihan and Lindsay Mizer

Contents

Money, money, money

What is money, and why do we need it anyway? Money is one thing that you receive for your hard work. You can earn money in many different ways. You can get a job or receive an allowance from your parents for doing chores around the house. Money allows us to buy the things we need, like food and clothes, and fun stuff like candy and toys!

Earning money

Most people get money by working. Companies or individuals pay people to make things or do certain jobs, such as fixing cars, cutting hair, teaching children, or programming computers. Some jobs pay more money than others. A few lucky actors, for example, earn millions of dollars for appearing in films and on television.

Inheriting money

Some people receive money when a relative or someone close dies and leaves money behind to them. This sum of money is called an inheritance.

A great idea

You might be doing something right now that will make you money some day. Are you always coming up with new ideas? Maybe you could make an invention that no one else has thought of. This could be something that saves people time or does the job of something else but with better results.

Athletes

How about sports? Are you a good baseball or basketball player? Successful athletes can be among the world's highest earners. They earn money by playing sports and also by endorsing products. This means companies pay them to wear certain clothes or use one brand of equipment. The companies hope this will encourage other people to wear or use these things, too.

Before money

People didn't always use the kind of money that we know today. Before money was invented, people grew their own food and made all the clothes, pots, and tools they needed. They built homes from wood or earth. If they wanted something that they could not grow or make themselves, they would swap or trade with other people. This is called bartering.

DID YOU KNOW?

Roman soldiers were sometimes paid in salt. This is where the word *salary*, which means wages, comes from.

Funny money

In the past, people have used cloth, metals, and food as money.

Dried tea (Tibet)

Bamboo sticks (China)

Cocoa beans (Mexico)

Swap shop

People still barter today. When you swap your toys or sports cards with your friends, you are bartering.

If the person you are bartering with does not want anything that belongs to you, you have to use money instead. Money can really be any object, no matter how strange, as long as it is valuable to the person receiving it.

Wampum belts made from clam shells (North America)

Copper rings (Nigeria)

Tobacco (U.S.)

In short supply

During World War II (1939–1945), Germany bombed the cargo ships that brought goods to England. This meant that items, like stockings, perfume, and candy were in very short supply. That made them valuable. People used to trade with these goods instead of using money.

Modern money

Look in your piggy bank or your wallet. It is probably full of coins and dollar bills. Modern money is not just made of pieces of paper or metal discs. We pay for things using credit cards or checks. You cannot even see or touch some forms of money because they exist only as information in a computer.

Paper money

You may have heard the expression "money doesn't grow on trees." You may not know, though, that money actually comes from cotton plants! Bills are printed on strong paper made from cotton. The pictures and letters on bills are made by printing plates, which transfer the pictures onto the paper.

Minting

Coins are made by stamping words and pictures onto blank pieces of metal. This is called minting.

Fake money

Photocopying bills is illegal. To keep people from passing fake, or counterfeit money, many bills have plastic strips in them. In daylight, these strips may look red, but when photocopied, they appear black.

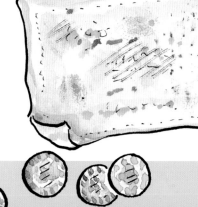

Credit cards

Adults can buy things using credit cards. These cards have a magnetic strip that stores information about the customer. This way, credit companies know where to find people when it is time for them to pay their bills!

Automatic Teller Machines (ATM)

Most banks have ATMs. These are computers that customers can use at any time to take out cash or find out how much money they have in the bank. To use an ATM, you need a special plastic card and a secret number called a PIN (Personal Identification Number). You will not get an ATM card until you are older, though.

Different ways to pay

Computers in banks hold information about how much money you have. If you have access to the Internet, you can send this info to other computers and pay your bills from home. Adults can also pay bills over the phone. This is called telephone banking.

Allowances

In some families, parents give their children their own money called an allowance. With an allowance, a kid can manage his or her own money. Some families expect children to earn their allowance by helping out around the house.

Good earners

Some of the jobs you might be able to do around the house:

Loading or unloading the dishwasher

Cleaning the house

Babysitting a younger brother or sister

Mowing the lawn

Cleaning a pet cage

Vacuuming

Taking out the trash

Setting the table

Extra money

You may be able to earn extra money by doing extra jobs. You could offer to clean the goldfish bowl or wash the car, for example. Remember, the jobs should be ones that your parents think need to be done. Hopefully, they are jobs that you enjoy as well!

Budgeting

If you get an allowance, it is tempting to spend it all at once. If you do, you will never save any money for large items. A better idea is to plan a weekly budget.

- Figure out what you need to spend each week on routine things.
- Look at how much you have left over. Decide how much you will save for special occasions like buying vacation souvenirs and birthday presents.
- Remember to save some money for emergencies.
- Try not to borrow money to pay for something. Wait until you have saved the money yourself.

Bank accounts

If you want to save part of your allowance, what do you do with it? You might want to consider opening a bank account. That way, you won't be tempted to spend it, and you won't lose it. The best thing about banks is that they pay you extra money on the money you save. This is called interest.

How to choose a bank

Choose the right bank for you. Ask the bank teller these questions:

- How much interest will the bank pay me?
- Is there a branch of the bank near my home?
- Is the bank open after school and on weekends?
- How much money do I need to put in, or deposit, to start my account?
- How much money can I take out, or withdraw, at one time?

Open sesame!

To open a bank account, you need to go to the bank with your parents and fill out an application. The bank will need some form of identification, usually your social security number. You will also need some money to put into your new account. Most banks give you a small book to record your deposits in. You need to take this to the bank every time you want to deposit or withdraw money.

That's interesting

When you put money in a bank, you are actually loaning the bank money. In turn, they pay you interest on what you have in your account. It works like this: imagine Piggy Bank pays 5% interest. If you save $100 for one year, the bank will give you an extra $5.00, and you'll have $105.00 total.

Bank statement

PIGGY BANK

Sarah Hamilton — Account No. 325463247

Date	Deposit (+) / Withdrawal (-)	Balance
June 14	$2.50 +	$2.50
June 18	$1.25 -	$1.25
June 21	$3.00 +	$4.25
June 24	$1.00 -	$3.25
June 28	$3.65 +	$6.90
July 2	$2.00 +	$8.90
Interest payable	$0.25 +	$9.15

Stocks and shares

One way to make more money is by buying and selling shares of stock. Businesses sell small parts of their companies called shares to raise money. By buying shares, you will get to own a small part of a big company. Although this sounds good, remember that millions of other people own shares, too, so one shareholder usually does not have much power!

How shares work

If the company does well, the value of the shares increases, then they can be sold for more than they were bought. If the value of the shares decreases, they will be sold for less than they were purchased.

Savings bonds

You may have received a government savings bond as a gift. A savings bond means that you are actually lending money to the U.S. government. A savings bond is purchased for half the value shown on the bond. A $100 savings bond, for example, has been purchased for $50. After a certain amount of time, you can turn in the bond and earn the full value--in this case, $100. That's because the government pays you interest on the money that you lent them.

Stock markets

Shares of stock are sold in places called stock markets or stock exchanges. The biggest stock exchanges are in London, New York on Wall Street, Tokyo, and Hong Kong.

You can find the price of a company's shares by reading the business section of daily newspapers or by looking on the Internet. The companies are grouped together according to what they make or sell.

This is the price of each share on a particular day.

RETAILERS
Funky Fashions $18.25 + $2.50
Casual Knits $17.25 - $0.25

This shows how much the price of the share has gone up (+) or down (−) during the day.

DID YOU KNOW?

Buying shares of stock can be risky. Ray Kroc used to own the fast food chain, McDonald's™. He lost over 40 million dollars in one day when the value of his shares fell!

Be a Wall Street whiz kid

Do you think you could make money by buying and selling shares? A fun way to practice is by playing a game of Virtual Stock Exchange. You can play this game on your own or with a friend. First, you will need to do some research to decide which companies you want to invest in. Then, get ready to play.

How to play

- Imagine you have $1,000. You can use all that money to buy shares in a single company, or you can buy a small number of shares in lots of different companies.

- Use the stock prices in newspapers to help you choose. Have an adult check that you have not overspent.

- Set a time limit of one to three months. During this time, you can buy and sell as many shares as you like. The more money you make during the game, the more shares you can buy.

- At the end of the game, you must sell all your shares and add up how much money you have made (or lost!).

Helpful hints

- Check the value of your shares every day. If the price of your shares goes up, consider selling them quickly to make more money. If the price falls, you can either sell your shares or hang on to them and hope that the price goes up again before the game ends.

- Choose some companies that make things you and your friends like, such as your favorite clothing store, music store, or fast food restaurant. If you know the company is popular, chances are the company will do well, and the share price will go up.

- Try to find out what other companies sell or do. This will help you guess if they are likely to do well. For instance, if you hear a weather forecaster say that it's going to be a cold, wet summer, it would be wiser to buy shares in a company that makes umbrellas than one that makes ice cream!

Earning your own money

So, you want to earn some money on your own? Discuss some ideas with your parents. They will probably support you and will help you find friends and neighbors who will pay you for the jobs they need done.

Odd jobs

You can begin by asking your neighbors if they have any jobs for you to perform. You might suggest washing their cars or mowing their lawns.

Extra! Extra! Read all about it!

If you are allowed to be out on your own, you might get a job delivering newspapers. Be warned, this can be hard work, especially on the weekend when the newspapers include lots of extra sections! On the plus side, lifting all that weight and walking in the fresh air is bound to get you in good shape.

A way with animals

If you like animals, you could offer to take care of a neighbor's pet while he or she is away. You could also walk dogs on a regular schedule.

Green thumb

If you have a green thumb, you could offer to water a neighbor's plants. Make sure you get good instructions. You don't want to drown his or her plants with too much water.

Yard sale

Is your room full? You can sell your old toys in a garage or yard sale to make money. You could also take things you no longer use to a resale shop. To sell large items, you can advertise in the newspaper or on the Internet—with your parents' permission of course.

Start your own business

Starting your own business can be rewarding. Not only will you earn money, but you will also learn how to organize your time. To get started, you will need to decide whether to start your business alone or with a friend. You will also need to decide whether you want to offer a product, like cookies, or a service, like dog-walking.

Choosing a theme

- Valentine's Day could be a perfect opportunity to make and sell products such as cards or cuddly toys.
- Christmas is a good time to offer products, too. Consider making wrapping paper or baking Christmas cookies.
- Summer is an ideal time to start a lawn service. You could cut your neighbors' lawns and water their gardens.
- In the winter, you could offer to shovel snow from driveways and scrape ice off of car windshields.

Seasonal work

Do you want to offer your business all year round or just for certain months of the year? If you offer a service such as lawn mowing, you will work only when the weather is warm and sunny. If you offer a dog-walking service, you will be able to work all year round.

Getting started

Think about the following questions first:
- How much will it cost you to buy the materials to make your product?
- Who will make your product? If someone else is working for you, how much will you have to pay them?
- How many items will you make?
- How long will it take to make the products?
- How will you take orders and deliver the products to your customers?

Your customers

Before you start your business, you need to think about some very important people—your customers. Who are you going to sell to? Do they need what you are selling? What price are they willing to pay? What extras can you throw in to make your business appealing?

Finding your customers

Where will you sell your product or service? Think about where your customers are and take your product or service to them. If you are selling to friends, try taking your product to school, if that's permitted. If you want to wash cars, ask your parents to join you and knock on the doors of neighbors who own cars.

Advertising

How will you sell your product or service? You can let people know about your business by advertising. If you are offering gardening or babysitting services, hand out flyers or business cards to family and friends. Never approach strangers. Be sure to include information about your business like what kind of service you are offering, your fee, and how customers can contact you.

Dawn and Doug's Dog-walking Service

Do Pooch, Polly, and Bruno need walking?
We will walk your dogs for one hour each day.

If interested, call Doug at 555-1234.

Being reliable in business

Whatever business you choose, make sure you deliver what you promise. If you don't, your customers won't trust you. If you say you will pick up a dog at 9 a.m. for its morning walk, make sure you are on time. Better yet, be there early.

The competition

The other important people you need to get to know are your competitors. These are people or businesses who offer products or services similar to yours. Find out as much as you can about your competitors. Research how much they charge and what people like and do not like about their product or service.

Beating the competition

How can you beat the competition? Here are ideas:

- Offer a product that is better in some way. Do your cookies taste better? Are your card designs cooler? Make sure you communicate these advantages to your customers.

- Sell your product at a lower price than your competitors. Before you lower your prices, make sure you can cover your costs and make a profit.

REMEMBER Make sure to communicate how your product is superior to the competitors.

A unique product

One way to beat your competition is to sell something that is different or better than your competitors. For example, Clarence Birdseye introduced a different product in 1925—frozen food! His brand is still a top-selling product today! You could also try to think of a way to improve an existing product to make your version better.

A good reputation

A good reputation is an important factor in a successful business. If people find that your product or service is better they will prefer your business over someone else's. They probably will even tell other people about it! Try to give your product a memorable name as well. That way, people will be able to easily remember it!

Your millionaire fantasy

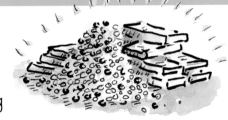

If you start your business now, one day you could own a huge corporation and have lots of people working for you. Here are a few stories of people who made their millions early in their lives and how they spent their money.

Computer millions

Bill Gates started making computers when he was just 20 years old. He is now one of the richest people in the world. He does not keep all of this money for himself though. Bill Gates is a philanthropist. Each year he donates millions of dollars to charity.

TV star millions

Some of the richest people in the world are music and movie stars. Most stars who make millions are talented and lucky. They are also smart enough to manage their money well.

A stingy millionaire

Hetty Green was one of the world's richest women. She was so stingy that she ate cold porridge so she did not have to spend money heating it up!

How to spend your millions

It's fun to think about how you might spend your money if you made millions! Here are some fantasies about what you might spend your money on.

You could buy your mom the world's most expensive diamond. It was sold in 1995 for over $15,000,000!

You could have a party for all your friends and family. The world's most expensive party was held on July, 13, 1976, in Brunei. It cost $25,000,000!

What really matters

It can be fun to think about how you would spend a lot of money. But remember, all of the money in the world probably won't make you truly happy. The satisfaction of working hard, earning your own money, and learning to budget it responsibly will though!

Glossary

Advertising

A way of letting your customers know what you are selling. You can hand out flyers or business cards to help your sales.

Balance

The difference between the money you put into the bank (deposit) and what you take out (withdraw).

Bartering

Trading without using money by swapping things that others want.

Budget

A plan of how much money you have and how you will spend it.

Competition

The other people or companies who sell a product or service similar to yours.

Credit card

A card that allows you to buy things now and pay for them later.

Customer

A person who buys your product or service.

Deposit

Placing money into a bank account.

Employee

A person who works for another person or company in return for a salary.

Employer

A person or company that pays someone money in return for their work.

Endorsing

Expressing approval for a product or company.

Interest

Money a bank pays its customers for letting them use their money.

Minting

Making coins by stamping disks of metal.

Profit

The amount of money you make from selling a product after you have subtracted how much it cost to make.

Salary

The money or wages paid by employers to their workers for doing a job.

Shares

Equal parts of a company. Each part has the same value.

Stock exchange

A place where shares in companies can be bought and sold.

Withdrawal

Removal of money from a bank account.